Spectacles of Stepantsminda

MOUNT KAZBEK AND GERGETI TRINITY CHURCH

A TRAVEL PHOTO ART BOOK

LAINE CUNNINGHAM

Spectacles of Stepantsminda

Mount Kazbek and Gergeti Trinity Church

A Travel Photo Art Book

Published by Sun Dogs Creations
Changing the World One Book at a Time
Print ISBN: 9781951389079

Cover Design by Angel Leya

Copyright © 2019 Laine Cunningham

All rights reserved. No part of this book may be reproduced in any form or by any means, electronic, mechanical, digital, photocopying or recording, except for the inclusion in a review, without permission in writing from the publisher.

THE TRAVEL PHOTO ART SERIES

Ruins of Rome I & II
Along the Via Appia
Garden City Garbatella
Ancients of Assisi I & II
Captivating Capri
Milan Cathedral
Treasures of Turin
Panoramas of Portugal
Linger in Lisbon
The Splendors of Sintra
Spectacles of Stepantsminda
Grandeur in the Republic of Georgia
Tableaus of Tbilisi
Original Old Tbilisi
Marvels of Mtskheta
Paragons of Prague
Hidden Prague
The Pillars of the Bohemian Paradise
Lidice Lives
Terezín and Theresienstadt
Flourishes of France
Portraits of Paris
Notre Dame Cathedral
The Beauty of Berlin

PUFF

OUTPOST

COMBUST

FOOTFALL

AMPLIFIER

BACKYARD

TICKLE

TRANSECT

KEYHOLE

SMAUG

TAXI

ECHO

BUTTERFLIES

AWAKE

THE SHIRE

MORTAR

TRANSIT

QUAKING

SCRAMBLE

POPOCATEPETL

MINT JULEP

LOWERING

WEEPING

About the Author

Laine Cunningham leads readers around the world. *The Family Made of Dust* is set in the Australian Outback, while *Reparation* is a novel of the American Great Plains. Her travel memoir *Woman Alone* appeals to fans of *Wild* and *Eat Pray Love*.

Novels by Laine Cunningham

The Family Made of Dust

Beloved

Reparation

Other Books by Laine Cunningham

Woman Alone: A Six-Month Journey Through the Australian Outback

On the Wallaby Track

Seven Sisters: Spiritual Messages from Aboriginal Australia

Writing While Female or Black or Gay

Ruins of Rome I & II
Along the Via Appia
Garden City Garbatella
Ancients of Assisi I & II
Captivating Capri
Milan Cathedral
Treasures of Turin
Panoramas of Portugal
Linger in Lisbon
The Splendors of Sintra
Spectacles of Stepantsminda
Grandeur in the Republic of Georgia
Tableaus of Tbilisi
Original Old Tbilisi
Marvels of Mtskheta
Paragons of Prague
Hidden Prague
The Pillars of the Bohemian Paradise
Lidice Lives
Terezín and Theresienstadt
Flourishes of France
Portraits of Paris
Notre Dame Cathedral
The Beauty of Berlin

The Zen of Travel
The Zen of Gardening
Zen in the Stable
The Zen of Chocolate
The Zen of Dogs

The Wisdom of Puppies
The Wisdom of Babies
The Wisdom of Weddings

The Beautiful Book of Questions
The Beautiful Book for Dream Seekers
The Beautiful Book for Rebels
The Beautiful Book for Women
The Beautiful Book for Lovers

www.ingramcontent.com/pod-product-compliance
Lightning Source LLC
Chambersburg PA
CBHW041321110526
44591CB00021B/2863